better together*

*This book is best read together, grownup and kid.

a kids book about creativity™

by Sara & Stewart Scott-Curran

a kids book about™

Library of Congress Cataloging-in-Publication Data is available.

This book represents our personal experience and thus is not intended to be representative of every form or example of creativity as it applies everyone else.

A Kids Book About Creativity is exclusively available online on the a kids book about website.

To share your stories, ask questions, or inquire about bulk purchases (schools, libraries, and non-profits), please use the following email address:

hello@akidsbookabout.com

www.akidsbookabout.com

ISBN: 978-1-951253-05-9

Printed in the USA

To Skyler Everly,
the most creative person we know

Intro

Have you ever been told you aren't creative? Maybe that's even something you tell yourself. What if it simply wasn't true? What if it's the most sneakiest lie you've ever been told?

Expression through creativity can not only improve your happiness and self-fulfillment, but it can be REALLY FUN, too!

But often, we either dismiss creativity as not important enough to talk about, or we just accept the notion that some people are born creative. And some just... aren't.

Creativity feels like a big word that means something different to everyone and everyone is RIGHT! If you don't think of yourself as a creative person, we're hoping that by the end of this book you will expand your definition of creativity and see yourself as a one-of-a-kind creative being!

Hello, my name is Stewart, and I'm an artist.

(Every time I say something, it's blue)

And my name is Sara,
and I'm not an artist.

(Every time I talk, it's orange)

BUT, WE'RE BOTH...

creative!

(When WE say something, it's purple)

And guess what?!

Spoiler alert:
You're creative too!

This is a book about **creativity.**

Creativity is like a...

SUPERPOWER

but one that everyone has.

We want you to unlock your creative superpower.

And learn how to use
it everyday...

in both

BIG

and SMALL ways.

When I was a kid, people told me that I wasn't creative.

And I believed them....

Because I wasn't the best at...

Drawing

Singing

Painting

Or writing stories.

Even my mom never hung my artwork on the fridge.

But when I was a kid,
everyone told me...

I was creative all the time!

Because I was really good at...

Drawing

Painting

Writing stories

And making things.

My artwork ALWAYS won a prize!

Most people think you're either born to be good at those things...

or you're not.

But, what if being creative was more than just...

Drawing

Singing

Writing

Or

Painting well?

What if there were

THOUSANDS THOUSANDS THOUSAN
USANDS THOUSANDS THOUS
SANDS THOUSANDS THOUS
HOUSANDS THOU
THOUSANDS THO
DS THOUSANDS THO
OUSANDS THOUSANDS THO
NDS THOUSANDS THO
DS THOUSANDS THOUSANDS T
THOUSANDS THOUSANDS T
ANDS THOUSANDS THOUSAND
HOUSANDS THOUSANDS THOUSAND
THOUSANDS THOUSAND
USANDS THOUSAND
HOUSANDS THOUSA

THOUSANDS THOUSANDS

of ways to be creative?

So many, in fact, that there is

more than enough to go around?

You might have already done some of them today...

(Still me Stewart in blue)

Whether you realized it or not.

(Still me Sara in orange)

Creativity

is

just

being

Taking your own approach to something,

bringing your own point of view,

and doing something in a way only you could do it.

are CREATIVE!!!!!!!

Did you choose your own outfit today?

Did you eat breakfast today?

Did you hang out with a friend this week?

Did you play a sport today?

Did you do any math lately?

Each of these can be done in a **CREATIVE** way, unique to you.

You could have one-of-a-kind style in your outfits.

Or maybe you put BBQ sauce on your breakfast.

Maybe you invented a new game with a friend.

Did you think up a new move to try during soccer?

Did you solve a math problem in a new way?

All of these are examples of...

creat

ivity!

And if you did even one,
that makes you creative.

Can you think of some
other ways that
you can be
creative?????????????????????????

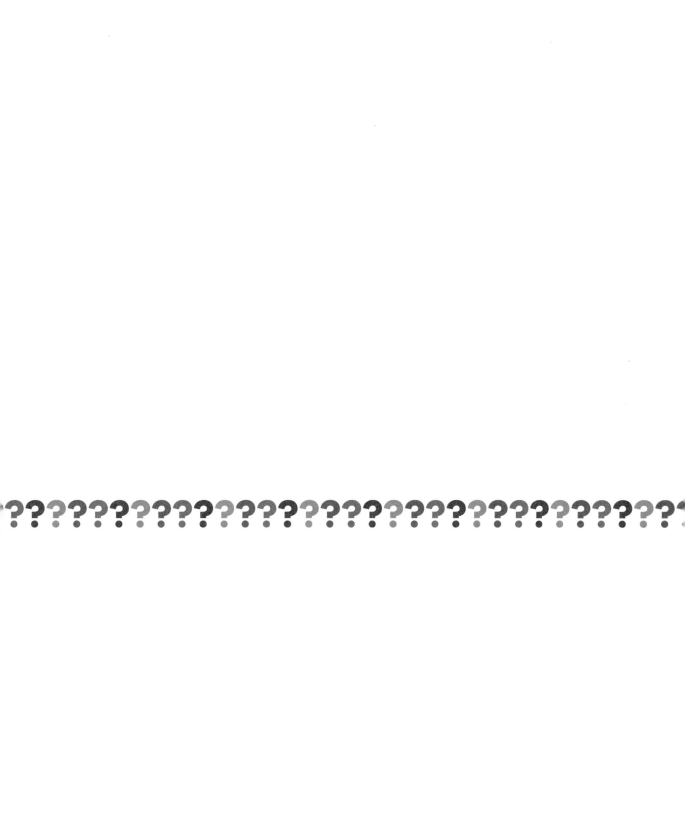

What about...

Tying your shoes in a different way?

Posing for a picture?

Dancing in public (even when no music is playing)?

Not being afraid to get messy or weird or be super silly?

What about...

**Making up new words
to a song?**

Only walking on the squares,
not the cracks of the sidewalk?

**Making your hair into a shampoo
Mohawk during bathtime?**

Pretending the sand at the
playground is lava?
(be careful not to touch it or...)

You are unique, creative, and original...

and that is...

AWESOME!

Showing who you are in big and little ways...

is an expression of your truest, most creative self.

And when you do that,

the world is a happier

and brighter place!

Outro

Congratulations! You are a creative original! High Five! We hope this book has shown you that there a million ways to be a creative person, and they all have value!

Now that you know how big, awesome, and all-encompassing creativity can be, here are some things you can chat about with your kiddo to help their creativity shine. Start with your experience with creativity when you were little. Talk about how each of you express your creativity now. Count all the times in a day you use your creative muscle.

Or try doing some really practical things together. Make dinner a new way, or even have breakfast for dinner! Work together to solve a problem, build something, take some pictures, or make slime! Anything that will get you thinking in a new way.

Remember, YOU ARE CREATIVE!

find
more
kids
books
about

belonging, feminism, money, racism, depression, failure, gratitude, adventure, cancer, body image, and mindfulness.

share
your read*

*Tell somebody, post a photo, or give this book away to share what you care about.